DATE DUE

THE SPITE HOUSE

THE SPITE HOUSE

poems

ELIZABETH KNAPP

ISBN 10: 1-936196-06-9
ISBN 13: 978-1-936196-06-7
LCCN: 2011923559

C&R Press
812 Westwood Ave.
Chattanooga, TN 37405

www.crpress.org

Cover painting by Johan Lowie (*The Recurring Dream*, oil on canvas, 24"H x 32"W)
http://www.johan-lowie.com/

Author photo by Robert Eversz

Cover design by Jamie Iredell

Acknowledgments

Grateful acknowledgment is made to the following journals and publications in which these poems have appeared, some under different titles:

Agni Online: "Self-Portrait Triptych: Amputee"

Barrow Street: "The Dead Sea"

Best New Poets 2007: "Betray"

Beyond the Valley of the Contemporary Poets 2003. "Spiderman Converts to Buddhism," "Spiderman on the Paradigm of Marriage"

Crab Orchard Review: "Spiderman Considers a Career Change"

CUTTHROAT: "What Clytemnestra Saw"

DMQ Review: "Eurydice's Lament," "Postscript from Hades"

Flights: "The Bone Church," "Self-Portrait Triptych: Japanese Stripper"

Iron Horse Literary Review: "Crocus," "The Crossing," "Self-Portrait Triptych: Garbo"

The Laurel Review: "The Garden"

The Massachusetts Review: "Intimacy"

Mid-American Review: "The Burning Bush," "Lost Letter III," "Lost Letter V"

Post Road: "The Plum Tree," "Uninvited Guest"

RHINO: "On Running into Jorie Graham in a Bathroom Stall at the Armand Hammer Museum in Los Angeles, or the Poem I Always Wanted to Write about Antigone"

Washington Square: "Lost Letter II," "Lost Letter IV"

Thanks to my teachers, April Bernard, Nancy Eimers, Thomas Sayers Ellis, Jane Hirshfield, Richard Katrovas, Anne Marie Macari, Bill Olsen, and Daneen Wardrop, for their invaluable insight and guidance.

Thanks also to my friends and close readers, Gina Betcher, Mark Conway, Jenny Factor, James Allen Hall, Kirun Kapur, Alex Kinnebrew, Cody Todd, and Bernie Zirnheld, for their encouragement and fellowship.

Special thanks to Bob Funk and Hood College for their generous support of this book, and to Jamie Iredell, Chad Prevost, Ryan Van Cleave, and everyone at C&R Press for making it a reality. Many thanks to Johan Lowie for the use of his painting on the cover. My enduring thanks to Richard Jackson for having selected the book.

Finally, to Robert Eversz, my deepest gratitude and love.

Contents

I

The Crossing

Lago di Como

I didn't make the connection at first, sun-stroked
        and weary of beauty, all that overripe lushness,
    the panoramic vistas, as the copper

we scraped from our pockets plinked in the alms
        box and incense snaked into our lungs, our hair.
    or perhaps I never saw it, ferryman

to my own soul, lugging my own shadow
        down winding cobblestone, past windows
    framed by boxed geranium, until we stopped

in front of the church and decided for once
        to enter. Inside, he left me to my own devices,
    withered and wary of inspiration, yet another

crumbling medieval relic in a picturesque Roman
        town. After mass we walked back to our room
    and watched the ferries cross the mirrored lake,

stitching and restitching the surface, remaking it,
        the thread of a threat or promise in their wake. I thought
    I ferried myself alone, but what I didn't know

was that there was a god in my boat, coxswain
        at the stern, ghost-love forever propelling me
    forward, whether or not I chose to believe it.

I didn't see the fresco until later, after I
        had arrived back home and organized
    my trinkets—downloaded photos, train tickets,

glossy brochures of villas we never set foot in,
all the churches we never saw, save one—
half-mast, hunched by the burden of grace,

St. Christopher carries the infant Jesus to the other
shore. From a distance, he is Christ himself,
entreating us, offering us safe passage,

hulled in the ribs of a sainted giant, whose sole
Sisyphian task is to keep our weighted souls
from drowning, a Charon steering in the opposite

direction, across the frothy, whitecapped lake.
It is only now that I can see him clearly, what he
means to us: at the harbor, in the moonlight,

love courted then cornered us.

The Dead Sea

From Amman we took a taxi to the Dead Sea. You wouldn't look at me, eyes fixed on the desert we hurtled through, rougher now the terrain, vaster now the hole I fell into, layer upon layer of sand over sky, sky over sand, your hand never once seeking my hand, the driver hidden behind dark glasses, the earth hidden, the sea… I remember now how unprepared I was, my breath dropping with each turn, my entire body quaking. From where did such violence begin? No sign of life, not a single bird or thirsting tree, even the sun could not rise, a mottled star galaxies away. I had to shout to be heard: *Leave me, let me be.* And now with biblical sweep, the first glimpse: oily with a sheen that so shattered all looking. Nothing could have prepared me.

Lost Letters

I

Do you remember? We were in a room
with the blinds drawn, a ceiling fan
slicing the hour into quarters, a tomb-
like stillness in the air, your open hand
resting on the pew of my back, beyond prayer.
Outside, the dusty static of a muezzin's call.
You kneeled over me, in the dark, the bare
tips of your fingers rehearsing all
parts of me you've touched. This
never happened, I tell myself now.
I've made the whole thing up—from the bliss
of that first lie to the years we somehow
vanished—you, a ghost between lives,
I, one of your many imagined wives.

II

Everyone lies. You heard but then forgot
the sound truth makes as it scuffles to the door
to be let out. You let it go like an unloved pet, not
caring if it ever came back, wiped paw prints from the floor,
then slept in your furless bed, innocent. Nights,
the lies kept you warm—their quilted seams
never showed a stitch, though time had worn them right
to the thread, a sheen to their satin lining. Still,
                          some dreams
troubled you. Waking, you refused to believe the ghost-
song in your head was your own voice echoed back to you,
high-pitched and terrible, the bile it left in your throat,
as you coughed up the last night's deceptions, true
to the lies you told even to yourself. They returned
not as strays, but as voiceless years that burned
                          and burned.

III

Have I confessed enough? My own lies caught
in my throat like starlight sucked by muses. I couldn't
form the words to describe it: years in California wrought
by silence, muffled by seasonless light. Time wouldn't
materialize. At the Port of Long Beach, ships moved
with the languor of summer, drifting in and out
of harbor, never docking long enough to prove
they were anything but ghosts. So we lived without
anchor, floating through west-facing rooms, sifting
the April sunlight for clues that somewhere it might
be snowing. Somewhere a plough was lifting
spring soil, the detritus of all we left covered by night.
I confess I remained silent. I confess time yearned
for a forgotten language we'd not yet learned.

IV

Fuck this form. Tell the story straight:
I was the lost child. He loved me.
Nights, across this city we wandered late,
getting high on graveyard walls where he
first tried to kiss me, the moon flung up
behind the paneláks like a stage set,
the dusky screen of stars, the night a cup
of headiness. Friends, I confess, I let
my imagination run away with me. Even
memory is a lie, colored by the anthem
of distance. I wanted to believe
I was lost. I purposely tried to lose him.
I knew I would return, this time alone,
my back to the river I never called home.

V

Some closets grow sacred until they become you,
until what's left unspoken runs through your veins,
erasing your every memory, until the only truth
is silence. You don't remember how you came
to see this life as the real one, not the life you left
behind, struggling to make sense of itself, the same
wordless ghosts you refused to feed, bereft
of their native language. Here they are again,
in the form of birdsong outside your window,
a melody so pure you'd forgotten the sound pain
makes when it opens, cracking like spring to show
you grief. Now the tulip tree across the street
has burst into a memory you will not repeat.

Spiderman's Angst

In the end, he decides, the scenery
    is unimportant—pitched on the balustrade

of the Brooklyn Bridge, the lights
    of Manhattan do not surprise him

anymore, the island's own constellation
    of stars, burning headlong across the Hudson.

He's had enough of playing good cop
    to the city, fed up with endless nights

swinging rapists over his shoulder,
    throwing arsonists back to their fires,

ridding Wall Street of corporate terrorists.
    Tonight he longs for a rice field in Malaysia,

the tip of an almond-eyed woman's tongue
    in his ear, something foreign and entirely sensual—

not sex, though sex would be nice,
    the shiver a spider might feel as he comes,

and the human side left to decipher it.
    No, something simpler than sex, simple

as a Sunday afternoon in the Hamptons,
    late July, a wife slicing sweet Maui onions

in the kitchen, and Etta James on the stereo:
    How deep is the ocean, how high is the sky?

The Bone Church

Rifling through a box of photos, I find a black-and-white snapshot of a pile of bones, human and mostly femurs, some of them pointed at the camera so that you can see their hollow openings, like the ends of flutes. The bones are from the Massacre of Sabra and Shatila, you tell me. From this, I construct the story: three hundred refugees are bulldozed from their homes, led to a narrow ravine and shot. What is left is the impression that you were once there, and somehow I have followed you. We move through the blasted landscape like hungry ghosts, picking at what's left of the bodies, our bodies, stabbing at the remains like crows bickering over a loaf of moldy bread. This is not a dream, yet somehow the memory precedes me, as if you had intentionally placed the photograph there, years later, for me to find. It reminds me of the chapel in Kutná Hora made entirely out of human bones. We walked past it once in early fall, when the Bohemian light cast silver shadows over the rooftops and cobblestones, before what was yours became mine, before the X-ray of your broken collarbone appeared in my files, its crack like the glaze of fired porcelain.

Uninvited Guest

Mid-September. First turn of the maples
like the underside of a kiss. Brush
of an angel's whisper. *Don't wait*

a second longer. Here, in this old house,
light bends a wishbone over the threshold
of a door. Night repeats its failures—

sky punctuated with stars, the comma
of a comet splicing the perfect sentence.
It wasn't yours: reflection of a woman

walking the cathedral's sunlit floors.
Someone else is speaking—not
the beloved, for whom Rilke waited

on Prague's reflected streets,
not the sighing of a window
as you gathered him in your arms—

what, after all, were you thinking?
It comes down to this: even your own
thoughts will betray you. They

were never yours, but the memory
of a collective conscience: hooded
figures on the horizon, Holofernes's

severed head bleeding in the basket,
as Judith spins her knife to point
the question back at us, the sheath

of history smeared. You watch
the images with less horror than
dumb amazement—the bodies

of a tyrant's sons sewn back
into a question, implicit and yet
unanswerable. Now someone

in the back row clears his throat,
as a woman in Gaza clears the gravel
from a grave. Husk of memory burning.

Pockets of autumn like signposts
along the highway. And still,
that swath of light above your door,

the guest that entered your blood
uninvited. You, who refused the warm
welcome of wine, even as you poured.

The Burning Bush

For weeks, I searched for a sign that it was over—
my rage or mourning, whichever came first.

I dug holes in the ground and covered the bulbs
with mulch. Then I waited. If something grew there,

I'd know I'd been granted. But earth doesn't respond
like that; there's nothing human in its language.

Words came to me, but they seemed the symptom
of something deeper. And then I saw it: blue-red

in the October sun, the color of a pomegranate
seed when light passes through it, or the amber-red

of a young Arbois, honey-red, yet bitter. It lit
the yard with the intensity of a dream, only I knew

its leaves weren't burning. Neither god nor prophet
it spoke to me, but what it meant I couldn't decode.

Reader, there are those who would say
I shouldn't address you directly, but this is not

that kind of poem—Frostian, dark, with a touch
of sardonic humor. Without you, I speak to the chasm.

Sublime, indifferent, the bush taunted me, its fire-
flecked voices I couldn't answer, its quivering vowels

slaking off heat. How was I to translate? I could say
it represented the untenable, the ineffable,

all that I had faltered or failed in (this gift to you,
my raspy hunger, the miniature graves I dug

in the hope for flower, my sad little conscience
pulling up weeds), but that would be untrue. Listen:

It's nearly winter and the bush is still burning.
In rage or mourning, I have failed you.

Intimacy

In a word: violence. From the Latin *intimus*: "inmost."
From there, according to Webster, see *intestine*. Consider
Brutus, son of Servilia, Caesar's favorite mistress, and the knife
he used to know the emperor in the most intimate and cunning
of ways: *You too, my son?* Or Signorelli, his real son lying dead
on the drawing room table, entering that beloved body through
the dissection of light and form. *Never let your brushwork show*,
David once said to his pupils. After Marat's assassination,
they called him in to paint the corpse, slumped in the funerary
bath, the body in rigor mortis still clutching the pen he used
to scrawl the name of his murderer. "The Pietà of the Revolution,"
it was called, implying the intimacy between death and politics.
If what is inmost cannot be seen, can it be touched by rage?
In a poem, one speaks from a place where two oceans meet,
a friend writes on one of my poems. I think poetic intimacy
is the fissure such joining creates. After it ended,
I experimented with the intimacy of sex, finding in each lover's
flesh a different kind of poetry, though my own body remained
the husk I carried out of one fire into the next, like fireweed,
like something that wouldn't be quelled. The last one wrote to me:
For what it's worth, you've known me in a most unique
and intimate way. For what it was worth, I'd learned nothing.
Seven years taught me not how to listen, to know each curve
of a voice, the bell at the back of the throat, what it wanted,
what it was really trying to ask, nor to see the soul for what
it might be—phantom windows of a farmhouse at dusk—
nor to enter that temple quietly, reverently. Instead, I learned
how to fake it. Intimacy was an art I invented for myself. And never,
not once, did I let my brushwork show. When it crept up on me,
benignly, tenderly, disguised as one come to ravish or save me,
I believed it, believed with all my slipshod heart it had something
to offer me—trust, perhaps, the quietude of knowing someone
cared enough not to kill me, and he, in turn, trusting me
with his life—all this to say: without threat of annihilation
there can be no intimacy. In its place, a wilderness smolders.
I would not become Caesar. From that inmost fire, I carved myself.

Betray

It began not
with a kiss of fury, the dark heavens opening
like labial folds to swallow Him complete,
whole, while Judas wept
in the shadows, fingering his promise
of gold, the pouch he
would kill or die for—

One of you
will betray me. No. It began with a kiss of indifference.
In the night, a single hibiscus bloom
unfolded despite me, despite
whatever storm would later
ravage it, despite my refusal
to water it, ignoring

its scarlet profusion,
its gaudy announcement of resistance.
Two days later, I knew, it would be gone.
Who can say with certainty
what Judas felt, as he lingered
in the garden after they
had taken Him away,

the tin shield
of the moon now polished and risen, the silver
knives of the olive trees glinting, the stones
now dumb and cold? No one cares
about Judas's own dark night of the soul,
as he slept on the bones
of his savior. I will

betray every flower
that opens for me, praying not for indifference—
the kiss of a wind that would flatten them
in caprice, or a frost that would ice
their tongues as they fold back to the dust
of my making—pray they die not in spite
but because of me.

II

The Spite House

This is the house that spite built.

This is the nose
that lay in the house that spite built.

This is the face
that wore the nose
that lay in the house that spite built.

This is the nun
who butchered the face
that wore the nose
that lay in the house that spite built.

This is the king
who raped the nun
who butchered the face
that wore the nose
that lay in the house that spite built.

This is the heart's klaxon horn
that warned of the king
who raped the nun
who butchered the face
that wore the nose
that lay in the house that spite built.

This is the grand salon unadorned
that houses the heart's klaxon horn
that warned of the king
who raped the nun
who butchered the face
that wore the nose
that lay in the house that spite built.

This is the inner curtain torn
that darkens the grand salon unadorned
that houses the heart's klaxon horn
that warned of the king
who raped the nun
who butchered the face
that wore the nose
that lay in the house that spite built.

This is the terror of early morn
that exposes the inner curtain torn
that darkens the grand salon unadorned
that houses the heart's klaxon horn
that warned of the king
who raped the nun
who butchered the face
that wore the nose
that lay in the house that spite built.

This is the virgin's bloody scorn
that heralds the terror of early morn
that exposes the inner curtain torn
that darkens the grand salon unadorned
that houses the heart's klaxon horn
that warned of the king
who raped the nun
who butchered the face
that wore the nose
that lay in the house that spite built.

This is the child of tragedy born
that inherits the virgin's bloody scorn
that heralds the terror of early morn
that exposes the inner curtain torn
that darkens the grand salon unadorned
that houses the heart's klaxon horn
that warned of the king
who raped the nun

who butchered the face
that wore the nose
that lay in the house that spite built.

Vandalism

Imagining still, as all poets invite us to, you can almost see Frost observing the vandalism and aftermath from that cabin above, wondering briefly whether these youths were, say, acolytes of Carl Sandburg, exacting revenge because Frost considered their hero poet second-rate. Sipping his tea, he rummages through his mind's deep storehouse for the metaphors that would provide context, that would find renewal in this destruction.

   —Dan Barry, *The New York Times*

In 455 A.D., the Vandals sacked Rome,
looting its treasures with remarkably
little violence, the whole operation
conducted explicitly for the purpose
of the acquisition of wealth, cleanly
and without significant bloodshed.
Now the old man looks on, and all
the rage, ire, and bitterness he could
not manage in life are resurrected
in these children, who know not what
they do, or where (the why, he muses,
is the eternal mystery, the eye of God
in a question mark), who may have read
"The Road Not Taken" once or twice
in high school and entered that night
through the storm door of memory,
armed with various accoutrements
of oblivion. What he really wonders
is if those kids see the irony—not the court-
ordered summer course in blank verse,
nor the thousands in fines and legal fees,
nor the retracted college acceptance letters
(no ironic injustice there)—but the fact that
they desecrated the spirit of the word
by ignoring his most precious gift (he'd rather
they'd stolen it), and besides this,
the alarm now installed on the stone wall
around the property makes obsolete
his metaphorical fences, the invisible nets
he cast between himself and the world.

The Tragedy

after the painting by Picasso

Child, there are other worlds
teeming inside you. The figure
of your mother, for instance,

half-mourner, half-corpse, forms
the outline of a bullfight scene,
a painting your father later

abandoned. The drama of the arena
once enthralled him—all that
gory color, lines the animals

horned in the dust, sickle moon
of the matador's sword—
but that was long before you.

Instead, he made you this:
space you can never fill,
an ocean of unspoken rage

between them, the sea's
recycled guilt, blame,
all that washes up blue

on the shore. But for you, child,
there would be no tragedy.
The tragedy is you were born.

Spiderman Considers a Career Change

Just ask Man Ray, and who was it
    who said, *Tears are liquefied brain?*

Rodin knew it, and so did Van Gogh,
    Picasso and his *Demoiselles d'Avignon*

were in on the secret so cloistered
    even superheroes couldn't unlock it:

Artists have more sex. Let's face it,
    hanging upside down from a web

isn't the most attractive position,
    and those graphite hairs that grow

thorn-like from his arms, his legs
    aren't helping the situation—

hot nights spent sleepless in his queen-
    sized bed, morning a sticky reminder

of his aloneness, a hunger beyond art,
    beyond reason. He dreams of painting

the autumn-haired waitress who pours
    his coffee every morning, the sleek seam

of her throat running down to the shadow
    between her breasts, down to where

his brush can't reach, a suffering so sweet
    it's addictive. Each night he paints her over—

spread-eagle on the afghan, in the bath,
    in fishnets, under a full-fleshed moon.

The Sense of Smell

after the painting by Jack Beal

What happens after a night
   of making love to a flower?
      Does it leave its breath

on her clothes, in her hair?
   The painting only shows
      the moment she has dropped

to her knees, nose-deep
   in the miracle, a tungsten
      moon reflected in the window,

its moonlike petals still unfolding,
   the belling of tropic perfume.
      Oh, but what isn't there—

in this story about loss even
   the story is lost. When she wakes
      on the carpet, a blank sketchpad

under her head, the moon-lamp
   now the sun, dawn breaking,
      it will be gone—a litter of petals

on the Persian rug, a trace
   of cloyed regret in the air.
      It is the aftermath she will

remember. And after that?
   Light reassembling like a fore-
      gone conclusion. The bitter after-

taste of bloom.

Eurydice's Lament

Love is not worth so much. I regret everything.
Me, tunneling my way toward oblivion.
As he turned back, stars flew.

Hell's air rank on my skin, while he's
above ground, weeping the notes
of the living. I regret everything.

By dawn, we would still be touching.
His come in my hair, the sweet dust
of our fear abated. Stars flew

through the window to warn us.
Morning crawled up the wall, but his singing
was more seductive than life. I regret everything.

What is there to forgive? That his lyre
would be my end, that the lilac-scented earth
would see the day stars flew

and open its bowels to embrace me?
His shadow marks every brimstone wall.
Is there nothing to forgive? I regret everything.

Psyche in Amman

What do I remember?
How huge his hand felt
as he led me through
  the marketplace. I remember

 dry heat, dust, December
sun rendering cold light
even colder. A hill flanked
  by cedar. That December,

 I knew I was truly lost,
grasping his hand to lead
me through the tenses
  to describe it—*now* lost

 in the consonant glare
of a future I couldn't see
to speak. So much light I thought
  I would drown, the glare

 a blindness, relief.
When I opened my eyes,
he was gone. What do I remember?
  Blindness, a relief.

Postscript from Hades

Thinking this might be my last season in life.
Thinking that death is not an answer, that the gull's
rinsed cry is a vowel that won't cast anchor,
won't serrate the gulf. Thinking that my love

was not meant for one lifetime, but for the stilled
valley of being, for the shifting of limestone,
for the fossilized breath of the dark. Thinking that song
is not suffered but shorn. Thinking that we peel

night from our bodies like salt. Thinking I can learn
to live with it, with this scull of a soul threading
the river Lethe. Thinking the last time I touched you
I crossed the last vespers. Mother,

I think the darkness has a name.
I think hell is my only lover.
I think, come spring, I will rise like a dead woman
carrying the blackened seeds of my heart.

Medusa in Hawaii

Once, in a riptide, I nearly drowned.
In that moment, no panic, no racing
heart to prove I was still alive,
as the current, like a god, took me under.

And, like a god, I resurfaced.
He was there, on the beach, gesturing,
a speck of wood I might have pulled
from my eye, a smudge of ink on the shore.

Wrested from the depths, carved
like a whelk from the sea's gilt floor,
I emerged, neck garlanded with seaweed,
a wreath of spite in my hair.

What Clytemnestra Saw

Her favorite daughter
offered to the gods

like an everyday farm animal,
so many bleating hearts.

Crafty, yes, but then so are the gods.

So many stupid humans,
their stupid human jobs.

So go on, fuck Cassandra
(unrolling her fine saffron carpet)—

and while you're at it, fuck the gods,
their dusty chariots and oversized cocks.

I have something else in mind.

She never asked for sympathy.
She asked for a bucket and a blade.

On Running into Jorie Graham in a Bathroom Stall at the Armand Hammer Museum in Los Angeles, or the Poem I Always Wanted to Write about Antigone

Maybe it was the hair, or the way she looked up at me as if from a tomb,
startled for a split second, before a smile spread like a crescent moon
across the gorgeous vacuum of her face. She looked almost pleased
to see me there, frozen in my spot, unable to move, like some stone
god struck dumb and gawking, before she cocked her head as if to say
Close the fucking door. So I did. I guess right then I was Antigone, buried

by my own shame, head in my hands in the stall next door. Should I have buried
my pride and apologized? Seconds later, I heard her emerge from her tomb
to wash her hands of me. But I lacked the will of Creon. I couldn't say
who I was in this story. Outside at the reading, a spotlight moon
lit her auburn hair. I watched the flyaways dance, Medusa-like, her stony
gaze boring into me. Here I go again, mixing myth. Reader, please

bear with me. The thing is, I always believed Antigone did it not to please
her brother, the gods, or even herself. It was Creon she wanted to bury.
When she crept out that night, beyond the castle walls, inside the ring of stones
they'd laid around her brother, she felt more alive than ever. The tomb
was the bed and the living flesh she left sleeping. Wrecked under a gibbous moon,
Haemon would wake to find her missing. If he asked her, what would she say?

Tell your king to go fuck himself, when he wasn't listening. Which is not to say
she wanted to die, but that she wanted vengeance. Later he would beg, *Please,
father, for the sake of the kingdom…* but it would be too late. The Theban moon
was already waning. By dawn they would find her hanged, her rage unburied,
even in death, an open challenge to her uncle. The world was a tomb
in Antigone's eyes. Neither love nor mercy could save her. Stone-

blind, like her father, Antigone died wedded to spite, while Haemon got stoned
on his grief. So the question remains: Who was Jorie in all this? I could say
she was the voice of the Chorus—her perfect indifference the silence of a tomb
once the last breath has been taken, each raspy poem a paean to the gods to please
their jealous natures—but who was I to remake her? All meaning lies buried
in wonder. After the reading, I watched her walk out to her ride, the L.A. moon

throwing shadows behind her. I heard her say to her companion, *Jesus, that moon will kill me tonight*. And so it did, dear Antigone. Like light from a dead stone, poetry reveals our passions. In this underworld, every line will bury its author. I went home that night wondering what I should have said when I walked in on her pissing. Part of me still thinks it pleased her, that moment between us when nothing was said, the bathroom a tomb

of failure. Now when I read her, I think her poems are trying to say (through background noise of the Chorus) *Forget trying to please them, the gods. Irreverence is your only prayer in the tomb.*

Spiderman on the Paradigm of Marriage

With great power comes great responsibility.
    As he left M.J. that November day, the skies

slating over with the onslaught of rain, his mind
    turned toward Odysseus: that's what he thought

as his ship left the harbor, as his bleached sail
    waved goodbye to the woman standing alone

on the quay, suffering in silence, powerless
    to stop him, powerless to bring him back

into their bed where Argos snored and snarled
    through dreams, where her loss was stationed,

rooted to the same emptiness she carried even
    while he was with her. What is war compared

to that hell? No wonder he invited seduction—
    a long-legged witch with a curtain of onyx

hair, tawny boys with tethered forearms, opium
    dens, an endless affair with the Mediterranean

itself—who could blame him? A superhero's
    hero. As he turned he could hear her crying,

the same recording playing over in her head:
    His only duty was to love me. M.J., sweet-

heart, get over yourself.

Self-Portrait Triptych

Garbo

I don't ask for her hieroglyphic eyebrows, or that gaze
        shuttered by sleepy lids, the lift that occurs just before

she parts her dewy Swedish lips and delivers
        a line like *I vont to be alone,* in a tone so perfectly

chilled it's delectable, nor do I ask for her mouth,
        pouty as this portrait is, the glamour that glossed her

right out of the picture, into Steichen's straightjacket
        frame, and announced her retreat from the limelit spectacle.

And her neck—that creamy slide into fantasy,
        collarbone, breast, lithe as Pavlova's when she tilts

her head back and laughs the cummerbund off her leading
        man, poor sod who never stood a snowball's chance

against a woman so mythic—I don't ask for that (this isn't
        a portrait for fetishists), nor hand, nor foot, nor arm, nor face,

nor any other part belonging to a siren, save two:
        her shoulders, twin burnished moons that rise

when she rises out of character and into pure starlight,
        their otherworldly aura, their glow from a previous era

when a flash of bone brought an audience to its knees,
        huddled before the mystery. Wry little sphinx, frosty

screen minx, tell me, would he love me more if I wore
        your silhouette? Who wouldn't trade the finger for a blade?

Japanese Stripper

Look: ravaged at desire's hem,
at the back of the catwalk,
    I glisten, skulking, waiting

to ignite, while suits sipping
sake from bamboo baskets
    bump knees under the table,

loosen silk ties. I fix them
hard with the red split
    of my smile, slink like I

was born to (sinking),
my bones sleek as a bird's
    and bracing for the funeral.

Listen: burn me. Burn
the boredom of this being:
    night after night like a cat

under the hideous moon,
or the burn unit after midnight.
    Mercy bleeds like that.

Thongs-away. Seething, I bloom
like acid over writhing flesh,
    light one lipsticked tit at a time.

Amputee

It was in Frost's "Out, Out—"
        that I found it, imago of myself

as amputee, the Mansfield ridge
        like a saw in the background

and the Vermont sky clotting
        into dusk. Farm bells. Suppertime.

And the saw, *as if to prove*
        saws knew what supper meant,

grinding through sinew and bone.
        Though Frost tells it differently,

I imagine the boy said nothing,
        no *rueful laugh*, as the life poured

out of him and the others watched
        dumbfounded, numb. Something

tells me it was no accident.
        There is loss, and then there is

what the mind freely gives up:
        He must have given the hand. If I cut

the part of me that wakes
        every morning wondering

how I could be whole—
        arms and legs intact, vertebrae

still stacked along the track
      of spine, skull still bobbing

on its pliant stem—I'd leave
      another part dangling, ghost-

limb tingling where the heart
      once skid. Is it better this way,

body still remembered, while skin
      grows thin and taut over a loss

so clean it can never be replaced?

III

The Plum Tree

This morning in meditation, I thought
of what remains: my pain, for example,

as I sat in half lotus in the flickering
light of my altar, nag champa incense

curling in the air, my feet going numb
as each breath rose and fell with the waves

on the lakeshore some thirty miles away.
Sit through it, Ben said, *and it will pass.*

Others had taught the same: Ellen
on her deathbed, struggling to speak

through morphine, clinging to each
word, as though the sound of her own

voice could save her; Holly at the tattoo
parlor, holding out her right wrist

in offering, eyes closed, as blood mixed
with ink that was carefully wiped away.

Pain ended for both, yet something
indelible remained. Now, when I think

of you, I remember that week in early
April, Ash Wednesday, when every tree

on our canyon-cradled street burst
into paper-white flower. All but the one

outside my office window. Plum trees,
I think. On Good Friday, they came

to cut it down. I watched as they fed
it to the woodchipper, angry beast,

the silence still angrier after it was done.
The stump left a hole no living thing

could fill. When I exhaled, it took forever
to be over. Opening my eyes, I could see

the oaks on my new street, gesturing
to sky, offering their tapered branches,

black candelabras shaking out snow. Nothing
stays, I know. And yet, you are etched in me

the way silence is etched into every spoken
word, the way the unsayable looms behind

every unlocked door. *Come in*, it says, *remember
me. Winter has begun and you are ready.*

Hydrangea

Now it sinks in: days of unwashed
gray, cracked pavement where puddles
of melted snow collect, snarled roots

exposed to the sludge of last week's
thaw. And this, you know, is only
the beginning: Saturn still in tow.

Matchstick trees behind the garden
fence, and a dog, now yours but only
for the day, asleep beside the dead

hydrangea. Take what you can
and make use of it. The rest feed
to the god of hopelessness, who never

endures for more than one season,
however long you think it's been
since a touch scalded your tongue

and passion drew the frilly curtains.
Tonight, speak to the moon in French
and break out your set of fine Czech

crystal. There's one Duraflame log
sitting in the fireplace and a host
of reasons for burning alone.

Petals

It's a marriage of convenience, though you could say
to the sky, *I'm yours for a season*, for however long

it chooses to bed you in its shag of white fleece,
its goose down of glistening powder. A weekend

now two thousand miles away, after the last vows
had been taken and the petals thrown like shrapnel

to the wind, a boy you hardly knew traced
the outline of the tattoo on your hip with the tip

of his ringless finger. Did it sing as it singed
going down? You woke the next morning married

to wonder, eating wedding cake for breakfast,
like Marie Antoinette, hungover. May the crumbs

nourish you this long and fruitless winter, even
as they fall, mute and wanting, to the ground.

Open Field

Someone has asked you to write about
angels, the quiet fractals wisping
sideways down your street, numinous

and steady, tender, unrelenting. Here,
they call it lake effect, though "lake"
is really a misnomer, as you've stood

on the brink of that saltless wonder,
on the dunes in September, well before
a single angel ever swelled from its vast

unsleeping shore. It is the god, and these
its minions, covering you, courting you,
burying you alive. They say death

by freezing is a most pleasant experience,
a delicious warmth spreading through
the body, the moment before consciousness

ends. *And a host of angels descended
from the heavens.* Winter won't kill you,
you know, though you may want it to,

though you may walk out one night,
numb to your life, bitten by degrees
too cold to ever succor and languish

in a open field of snow, an unbeliever,
a heathen in the midst of all that perfect
terror, benighted, yea, reborn.

The Elm

When I looked up from my reading,
it had stopped snowing. The bare arm
of an elm scraped the window. Then sun.

What had I been waiting for?
That moment when the minister
rises before the congregation,

his purple stole like a victory banner,
that moment when Christ appears
to his disciples in a cocoon of light?

What moved me was not light
in all its celestial hurry, the rush
of truth as it swells to the shore—

something darker had entered me.
I moved not because I was called to.
I moved because I was afflicted.

Lilacs

It was early June. You walked down your future street
in a Whitmanian rapture, with your borrowed lover,

who wore Mardi Gras beads and a half-baked smile
from his Ecstasy high the night before. He may have

held your hand. The heady scent was everywhere,
everywhere too the promise of flower, a borrowed

season in a borrowed land. Filched from your future
neighbor, a sprig of lilac, sweet purple dying in a vase

of water, or carefully folded into onion-skin paper
and shipped to Toronto for a homesick poet-friend.

Oh, Walt, what's the use in waiting? It's February
here in western Michigan, and not a single sign

of your heart-shaped leaves, no green to rend this ship
asunder, winter like a ghosted freighter anchored

in the mind, or a coffin carried on the shoulders
of comrades to the grave where we lay our vernal

hopes to rest, littered by sprays of lilac. What promise
can these offerings make us? *Desire, desire, desist.*

Lilies

The dead lilies you threw in the garbage
can't hear it, nor the streets, muffled
by March, its gray mouth filled with soot,

spewing quiet, nor the cat, curled
and dreaming of its own obsolescence,
nor the walls, windows, chimney, doors—

only your ears can draw out the faint
night scratches, the subliminal ticking,
the sense that something underground

is about to be reborn, someone once
buried is about to resurface—a child-
bride who spends half her life dying

and the other half waiting to die, though
this is your own morbid retelling. Myth
doesn't need you to hear it, it will go on

whispering in its ageless, garbled tongue
and you will go on believing in what lies
beneath it: *Listen, can you hear her crying?*

Crocus

It is mid-March, nearly spring,
    and I have wasted more than
        half the day thinking of what
    will not die, what will return
not as the bright opening
    of winter's end, but the pain
        of new bloom: crocus crowning
    the lawn, first flush of pink milk-
weed, seed pods sprouting pale green,
    while I fall somewhere between
        wanting to be over it
    and wanting it to kill me.
The old poet I loved in
    my youth says he refuses
        to give up his sorrow, that
    day after day, what does not
kill him makes him crave death all
    the more. I imagine him
        sitting alone in his stone
    cottage in Greece, the bleached light
falling in acres around
    him, writing a poem on
        the grief of watching the tide
    withdraw, how nights the moon burned
raw his longing. I think I
    understand what made him stay
        year after year in silence,
    only the blank sound of his
pail hitting the stone well or
    the cry of an owl through the
        black canvas of night. Returned,
    he arrives like the first shoots
of spring, not as harbinger
    but as witness: where language
        fails only hunger remains.

Scripture

Graffito: "Sadness Was Here"

The pronoun was the problem. You didn't want
to become your own first person, looking down

on yourself drinking with friends at the bar, laughing
as if you were one of them, not this disembodied voice

struggling to find its corporeal host, its sack of nerves
and flesh, the song the body makes when it opens.

So when you left the table to relieve yourself, opening
the door to the men's room stall, and read that one line

on the wall in a hand that could have been guided
by God or by a man adrift in his own loneliness,

you became *I*, *I* became *him* and *him* became all
that I had until then relinquished. At that moment,

it was scripture, and my body, no longer yours,
opened to a song before the advent of language,

before the primordial slime of pronouns began
to separate us—you from me, me from him, him

from the god of his sadness. When I returned
to the table, awakened yet unchanged, you greeted

me, pulled up an extra chair, told me to sit right there
and recount the story of my miraculous conversion.

Spiderman Converts to Buddhism

Sky-like, his mind has settled on emptiness.
    Lotus-style on his Casbah rug from Pier 1,

in his studio apartment on the Lower East Side,
    his third eye opens like a wound, as the mantra

of neon flickers through the blinds, car horns
    and sirens, the city's grit and grime, its slush

piles and suffering. He's immune to all that now.
    Stillness is his remedy, the hidden trump he deals

when he feels the weight of longing, a release
    from who he is in the world, or more precisely,

from who the world wants him to be; after all,
    who could blame Richard for turning his back

on the camera, shedding his shades for a hand-
    shake with the Dalai Lama (good PR if ever he

decides to return), and wandering knapsacked
    through the icy Himalayas? Countless times

he's considered pawning it all to the Iranian
    on the corner, buying a plane ticket to Bhutan,

and finding himself alone on a wind-ravaged
    peak, speaking Dzongkha, the stars etching white-

lined tracers in the sky. A lifetime ago, it seems.
    Now joy, a word so small yet miraculous, a circle

through which all karma passes, like the mouth
    of an infant, opens its sweet lips and swallows.

The Oak

First, a crack like the splinter of lightning,
as if the sky had clapped its hands
and opened itself to the dusk. I watched
a steady stream of cars snake its way
down my horseshoe drive, a tide
like a funeral procession. Turns out,
no one had died but a tree—an oak—
ravaged by drought or parasitic
disease, sprawling like a toppled
icon across the street, redirecting
the flow of traffic. I got closer,
bending down to where it had broken
open, a gash of rotten wood like teeth,
the head of a child in its hollow.
What will they do with it, I wondered,
and where to take the poem from here,
caught as I was in my own reflection,
seeing my own face in the scars
of a tree, a grief exposed to the blind
light of streetlamps, to the gawking
of random passers-by, to the dusk
congealing like blood at my feet.
I couldn't tear myself away. Then
it was no tree, but the felled weight
of suffering. Something had died
in me. For once, to look upon
that desiccated self—an ossuary
of broken limbs, a shattered crown
of leaves—and feel nothing but
the smooth balm of relief, a wave
of compassion rising. Meanwhile,
the oak lay ravaged on the six o'clock
street. Disgruntled drivers detoured.
I say this not to console or relieve:
There was no other way around it.

The Garden

I decided to look at it, once and for all,
my own loneliness, without judgment,

without accusation or pity, without
longing or shame, and see the same

mirror in the landscape reflecting
what I saw. Outside, to which my back

was turned, the oaks had sprouted
tight-fisted buds and sparrows marched

across the littered garden. *It's about
to happen, hang on.* I could go on

looking at it all my life, or I could turn
and walk into it, pick up the dead branches

over which a century of ice had burned
and tend the rows I never meant to abandon.

Spiderman on the Archeology of Memory

Once upon a time, in a lifetime far away,
    he remembers floating in a briny soup,

water so dense he could make love in it
    or walk across its polished oilskin, the primal

elements holding him up. Now experts say
    the sea is shrinking, sink holes swallowing

its seaside resorts, as nations spew into
    the Jordan River a biblical wave of sewage.

There, where Jesus first took the plunge,
    where Herod simmered in the royal hot springs,

 where a flock of Bedouin goatherds
    coughed up the dust of an ancient mystery,

there he felt his soul cave in, and there amid
    the fossilized scrollwork, in that pool of tears

he died himself, shedding one life for another, far
    from the clash of tribal warfare, the precarious

shift of ecological sands, in a town like Albany
    perhaps, or Milwaukee, or Denver, anywhere

with at least one good Thai restaurant,
    a decent library, four seasons, and a dependable

    supply of fresh drinking water.

Notes

"Lost Letter III": The lines "sifting / the April sunlight for clues" are from John Ashbery's "Self-Portrait in a Convex Mirror."

"Lost Letter IV": *Paneláks* are prefabricated Soviet-era apartment buildings found throughout the Czech Republic.

"The Spite House": A spite house is a building constructed to aggravate a neighbor, often by obstructing the view.

"The Sense of Smell": The lines "its moonlike petals still unfolding / the belling of tropic perfume" are from Robert Hayden's "Night-Blooming Cereus."

"Eurydice's Lament": The first line is from James Tate's "Coda."

The recipient of the 2007 Discovered Voices Award from *Iron Horse Literary Review*, Elizabeth Knapp has published poems in *Best New Poets 2007*, *The Massachusetts Review*, *Mid-American Review*, *Barrow Street*, and many other journals. She holds an MFA from the Bennington Writing Seminars and a PhD from Western Michigan University and is currently Assistant Professor of English at Hood College in Frederick, Maryland, where she lives with her husband and son.